PAIN, PRIDE AND POWER

SOURYA CHOUDHURY

Contents

1. The Warrior

A moonless night gives way to dawn,
The forces are at my door,
My time has come to go to war;
I see the aristocrats, I see the pawns,
Each of them wish to settle scores,
Unknown to me- what destiny has in store.

Donning my armour,
Unsheathing my sword,
I whisper a silent oath before the rays of the rising Sun;
To return victorious, or fall in battle,
A man true to his word,
Honour more valuable than a pyrrhic victory won!

Glancing at the mirror, I see my scars,
Anointing my skin like the sky's adornment with stars;
Some have healed from the blows and stabs,
Others still bleed, but weakness is just a farce!
Blades that have punctured my skin,
Arrows from each attempt to kill;

The blood, the pain and the torn flesh,
Have done nothing but strengthened my unshakable will!

Thus I commence on my final march,
Seeking power in a world where everybody wants to rule,
A cut-throat battlefield- only the fittest survives,
The thin line wanes further between genius and fool.
Comfort and fragility to be cast aside,
Breaking the shackles that held me back,
I do not know whether I'll make it to the other side,
Yet these prospects do not deter the warrior that I am!

2. My Will be Done

This day I stand on the edge,
Overlooking the battlefield before me;
The Art of War dictates patience and cunning,
What's ahead, rattles the knees of many!
The grind sharpens the Axe's wedge,
One that cuts through trees and throats with equal fury,
It's my turn to set the stage,
I shall not obey society's short sighted decree!

A missile set in motion is unstoppable,
Blazing ahead with relentless drive and momentum,
Locked upon the target from far, far away,
Once on its move, a formidable weapon!
A challenge is only as significant as perceived,
The 'pragmatic' are often prone to deception,
Impossible it is to make me retreat,
I've never done so since my inception!

The day has come for me to prepare for the charge,
While the thinker keeps thinking, the raider has already won,
Without mercy, through obstacles I barge,

Time does wait for those who can run-
I have no time for vain shows of arrogance,
There is a lot left for me to learn,
But that does not stop me from envisioning the future,
My Will soon to be Done!

3. Commander of Your Destiny

We start life with a blank slate,
A smooth and pristine chalk,
The stage yet to be set,
Free from envy, fear and hate,
The majestic tree commences its life as a mere sapling- a stalk.

The stopwatch starts with the very first cry-
Counting down till the day you die,
For every blink of an eye,
Hours, days, weeks, months, and years pass by;
You spend your first days dreaming, looking at the sky,
Beware! Don't let these priceless aspirations die,
For they'll take you far and high,
Soaring above the clouds like a hawk!

Live your life with no regrets,
Let there be no time for negativity;
Yesterday is dead and gone,

Wallowing in the past must never be your propensity!
If you deem yourself capable, you shall achieve the impossible,
Self belief- more powerful than rationality;
Plan for the future yet live in the present,
Don't let the opinions of others weaken your tenacity!

Neither go with the flow, nor fight against the current,
A warship's sails point towards its destination;
Don't let society and status quo restrain you,
Avoid falling prey to dangerous distractions;
Break the shackles of fear and self- pity,
Reject the chains- set your mind free,
Raise your flag as you march ahead,
Be the Commander of your Destiny!

4. Into the Cosmos

Ever since the beginning of time,
The commencement of human existence;
He's watched the sky,
As nights went by,
Wondered what's up there so high;
Farther away than his eyes could pry,
Observed the enthralling view through the window of his consciousness.
The ancient sages and the Greek philosophers,
Meditating upon the meaning the universe offers,
They lay on the grass and watched the stars,
Observed the celestial bodies from afar,
Squinted at them till they became a blur,
Wondering why that's how they are -
The more they observed, the puzzle of the universe became tougher!

Soon, came the breakthroughs of modern science,
A departure from the stagnant middle ages,
Intellectual minds were finally liberated,
From the shackles of custom; of religion- iron cages;

Telescopes to observe, equations to solve complex problems,
Astronomers and mathematicians replaced philosophers and sages,
Research to uncover the greatest mysteries,
An epic written down in history's pages.

With the arrival of the 20th century, technological prowess reached new heights,
The dream of flying became reality,
Traversing beyond the limits of the planet- once an impossible fantasy,
Entered the realms of practicality,
Scientific progress, already rapid,
Further accelerated by ideological enmity;
After the landmark breakthroughs of Sputnik and Apollo,
To explore the unknown became humanity's propensity!

We've come a long way since the beginning,
From the spherical – earth theory to sending missions to Mars,
Sending probes beyond Pluto, mapping the Kepler Belt,
Remote corners of the universe where energy is scarce.

The future holds immense progress and many
exciting breakthroughs,
With advancements in technology, stars millions of
light – years away will one day be considered close.
This is the result of humanity's unquenchable thirst
for knowledge,
Our journey into the Cosmos!

5. Memento Mori

Living without direction or purpose,
Taking life as it comes,
Embracing the vice of mediocrity,
Sailing amidst the doldrums,
Leisure time consumed by mainstream entertainment,
Wasting time arguing online with human scum,
Prioritising others' opinions before your own,
Inhibiting your own creativity and freedom.

An exemplary median on the statistic,
An example of how not to live one's life,
Sacrificing fulfilment for impulses and whims,
Succumbing to the distractions that are so rife,
Letting your senses dull- from a dagger of war to a butter knife,
Vision clouded by pessimism and gloom,
Overwhelmed by everyday strife!

Time waits for none, the clock keeps ticking away,
Each day- a step closer to the edge of the scythe

of the reaper,
A time when regrets will ripen, and remorse will overcome your frail self;
If change doesn't take place today, into the quicksand you shall only sink deeper!
So awaken the daring dreamer within,
Begin your journey towards glory,
With every tick of the clock,
The ship lurches closer to the jagged edge of the rock,
Wake up,
Wake up,
Wake up!
Memento Mori!

6. Soldier of Fortune

Get behind the wheel,
Tuck in your gun,
Hit the gas and drive into the setting sun,
You're a killer for hire; a wolf among an endless herd of sheep;
In it for the thrill,
It's a life on the run,
Just another sin that has to be done,
In the dead of the night, when the oblivious are sound asleep!

You're an honest rogue,
With little to hide,
In a world where every Dr. Jekyll has another side,
Virtue signalling was never your cup of tea;
It's just another deed,
To be done for the cash,
On the highway to hell, you just can't be

too rash,
Bloodied hands- just like any other, but not washed with hypocrisy!

Race and religion,
To you they don't make sense,
Every man falls to the Reaper's cadence,
Divided by borders, united by the darkness within;
Most live for distractions,
For what doesn't matter,
Idling away their time in meaningless chatter,
Waiting for life to wear thin.

You're sure of your mission,
The task at hand,
A mercenary obeying their own command,
As the world sleeps beneath a blood moon;
Thy will be done,
Take aim through the sight,
A twitch of the trigger shall win you the fight,
Is it wrong? Is it right?-
Does it matter?

You're a soldier of fortune!

7. They Decide- You Suffer

When a child is born in our country,
Their future career is usually debated on,
Hand-picked by society from a couple of
'superior' options,
Anything else is looked down upon with scorn.
Brought up to be a memorizing-regurgitating
machine,
Forever compared to their 'high performing'
peers,
By elders who consider themselves oracles- no
matter what the measure of their own success;
From nosy neighbours and know-it-all
relatives;
Patiently enduring endless jeers!

At the age of thirteen, one is coerced to choose
a stream;
One must select science-or else be deemed a
failure; no matter what one's dream!
A form of learning driven by demoralization
and fear,

Snide remarks to break your self esteem;
A ramshackle endowment of education, sheer mockery of meritocracy,
Only the wealthy afford coaching while the rest fend for themselves,
A system that caters solely to the cream!

The Gates of the University are drenched in the blood
Of every student who took their own life,
The revenue of coaching institutes wrapped in the shroud,
Carefully trimmed with a bloodstained knife!
Brainwashing from birth, indoctrinated with hypocrisy,
Taught 'facts' that defy the raw statistics,
They deny the urgent need for reform,
They delay the solution, the issues they never shall fix...

Your fate is not completely in your hands,
Although hard times make you tougher;
Who gives a damn about the voiceless at the bottom of the hierarchy-
They decide...
You Suffer!

8. Adapt

Trapped in the churning gears of the machine,
Coerced to live a life shaped by someone else's desire;
Undermined by the constrictive norms of a rigid society,
One that can't wait to light your pyre,
They force you into a rut, then let you fend for yourself,
Your well being is not their responsibility;
They have all the power and control,
Curbing your will is their default propensity!

In the name of your welfare, they feed you shameless lies,
"For developing life skills and ensuring holistic growth",
Do you think the old men-
Sipping tea at the council meetings, give a damn?
About the consequences of their plans and actions- and what happens to you henceforth!

An environment wrecked by overpopulation
and abuse of resource,
What's left is brutal, cut-throat competition,
No matter what happens to you, its not for
them to care,
Their intention is simply elimination!

Brought up in a culture riddled with
presuppositions,
Brainwashed and manipulated into idolizing
their idea of an 'ideal person',
"Let us tell you what to do 'cuz we know
better",
Stuck between a rock and a hard place,
You eventually fall prey to their coercion!
Rigidity and regression leave little room for
choice,
The self – serving deceived, enslaved by their
own greed,
You suffer the consequences of their karma,
But their authority and security remain
guaranteed!

At the end of the day, matters are in your
own hands,
You can fall prey to their Machiavellian tactics,
or hold your own against them,

Either swim or sink in the quicksand,
If you don't wish to lose your identity,
remember who you are!
The time for change will surely come,
None other than ourselves- can we expect the
agent of progress to be;
So until it's time to beat the victory drum,
All you can do is improvise, overcome, and
adapt!

9. Dawn of Dystopia

Waking up to the haze of the smoke from the pyre,
Corpses piled up, burning in the quagmire,
A million more casualties added to the statistic,
The sirens never stop screaming, the helpless asphyxiated, unable to speak;
Flattening the curve with an affinity for the vertical axis,
The monitor in the ICU flatlines with yet another anaphylaxis;
The deranged and the insane continue to be in denial,
Festivities that amount to mass suicide- they have rejected the contents of the lifesaving vial!

A nation in the choke hold of an invisible nemesis,
Struggling for breath, foot to the throat;
A system in the throes of paralysis,

Another life at stake with every positive
report.
The incompetence and arrogance of a hollow
leadership,
An administrative machinery that is crumbling
to dust,
A pseudo- conformist society blinded by
hypocrisy,
Grossly inadequate healthcare machinery,
weakened by rust!

Money gains value over human life,
When critical medication is syphoned into the
black market,
People oscillate between being paranoid and
utterly suicidal,
Leaving precautions aside, they continue their
escapades!
A gunshot to the foot in name of religion,
A race to the scythe of the grim reaper,
Betrayal intensifies as rallies continue amid
the carnage,
Every passing minute, into the bloodbath, we
sink deeper and deeper...

The prophesied apocalypse has long since
begun,

We take a step further in the direction of extinction,
Crematoria overflow with the remains of victims,
Hospitals loaded beyond their ability to function;
With every oxygen tank that is emptied,
Every life cut short by the deadly dyspnoea,
We sit back and watch the world burn,
Witness sunrise at the Dawn of Dystopia!

10. Trial by Fire

Rising at the crack of dawn,
Putting my head to the grind,
Time knows no leisure- nor do I,
I'm a ballistic missile- the target's always on my mind,
You can give me a thousand reasons why I can't,
I believe in the one reason why I can-
While you go with the flow, leading an ordinary life,
I choose to be second to no man!

Fighting the friction, navigating the chaos,
A graph with a constant positive derivative,
I don't believe in limits and obstacles,
As long as my effort is superlative!
You may call me a narcissist, decree me a fool,
Criticize me behind my back while I put my head to the grindstone,

Laugh at my setbacks, "I told you so";
Tell me which great warrior has never
broken a bone?

Building an empire is like eating glass,
I'm getting used to the taste of my own blood,
What doesn't kill me only makes me
stronger,
I'm not dead yet, and to kill me is hard!
The sharpest of blades are forged in the
hottest of flames,
Empires built by hands that never tire,
I shall either attain victory or fall in
battle,
There's no other choice-
This is my Trial by Fire!

11. Insurrection

I'm tired of wallowing in an ocean of mediocrity,
Trapped in a never – ending vicious cycle,
Drowning in a river that stagnated long ago,
Polluted with envy, deception and inflated ego,
That drains me of endurance and tenacity,
Viscous with the concentration of triviality!

I stand far away from the crowd,
I'm different from the rest, you may call me strange;
By myself I stand tall and proud,
Not confined to a narrow, compliant cage!

Pigeons flock together in hoards,
But the Eagle flies alone, soaring above the clouds,
Above the trivialities of snow and rain,
As I device a strategy within my brain;
Aloof and detached, you assume I'm not quite sane,

Spending time within the limitless realm of
my mind,
Detached and elusive yet addicted to the
grind;
Criticize me while you still have the grace to!

I don't give a damn about your narrow
perception of what I should be,
It's high time for you to realize!
I know you're trying to pull me down,
To your own level, out of jealousy and
insecurity,
But you'll eat my dust as you watch me rise!

The time has come for my transformation,
The ropes tying me back – to cut them clean;
To shower hate on me – you're most welcome,
Not a single graceless fibre shall remain!
You'll watch me ascend to heights you can't
even dream,
From your place down below, where you'll be
waiting to criticize yet another imperfection,
That doesn't prevent me from rising and
shining,
My victory is assured in the insurrection!

12. Pain, Pride and Power

A narrow passage leads to the hall of glory,
An unassuming portal to the gates of Sparta,
This steel does break many a man,
For whom the sacrifice is too difficult a barter.
Here train those who wish to ascend,
Who crave the metal bars of agony-
Self-made masochists dissatisfied with mediocrity,
Weary of instant gratification's common cacophony!
In a civilisation infected with a pandemic of softness,
Where people are restricted to their comfort zones;
The few that wish to metamorphose,
Are ridiculed, stereotyped and left to roam-
A society that separates it's scholars from it's warriors,
Has it's thinking done by cowards and it's fighting by fools,
We already see the impact- a sedentary lifestyle,
And norms that flout mother nature's rules!
Few take the decision to transcend this fallacy,
Fewer still have the resolve to stick to their plan,
For a man in pain falls like a deck of cards,
Not many have pleasure's clutches outran;
The grind is hard- it wears you to the bone,
Breaks you down and builds you up,

With every repetition, pain shudders through your nerves,
But the ecstasy that follows, sure fills your cup!
Those who walk this path unfazed,
By the million thorns that make them bleed-
The hundreds of hours of adrenaline and sweat,
The taunts of the ignorant, they do not heed;
They reap the sweet fruits of their labour,
A Greek God's physique that over others' does tower,
A mind as tough as wrought iron,
The results of this art of Pain, Pride and Power!

9 798888 151037

Printed by Libri Plureos GmbH in Hamburg, Germany